Baby

Illustrated by Sandra Meyer

COUNTRYMAN

Copyright of text © 2003 by the J. Countryman division
of Thomas Nelson Inc., Nashville, Tennessee 37214

Copyright of illustrations © 2003 by Sandra Meyer

Project Manager—Terri Gibbs

All rights reserved. No portion of this publication may be
reproduced, stored in a retrieval system or transmitted in any form by any
means—electronic, mechanical, photocopying,
recording, or any other—except for brief quotations in printed reviews,
without the prior written permission of the publisher.

All Scripture quotations in this book, unless otherwise indicated,
are from the New King James Version (NKJV) ©1979, 1980, 1982, 1992,
Thomas Nelson, Inc., Publisher, and are used by permission.

Designed by Left Coast Design, Portland, Oregon.

ISBN: 14041-0006-7

www.thomasnelson.com
www.jcountryman.com

Printed and bound in Italy

What joy is welcomed like that of a newborn child?

Caroline Norton

> He will gather the lambs
> with His arm, and carry
> them in His bosom.
>
> ISAIAH 40:11

Dear Father,
hear and bless
Thy beasts and singing birds,
And guard with tenderness
Small things that have no words.

Unknown

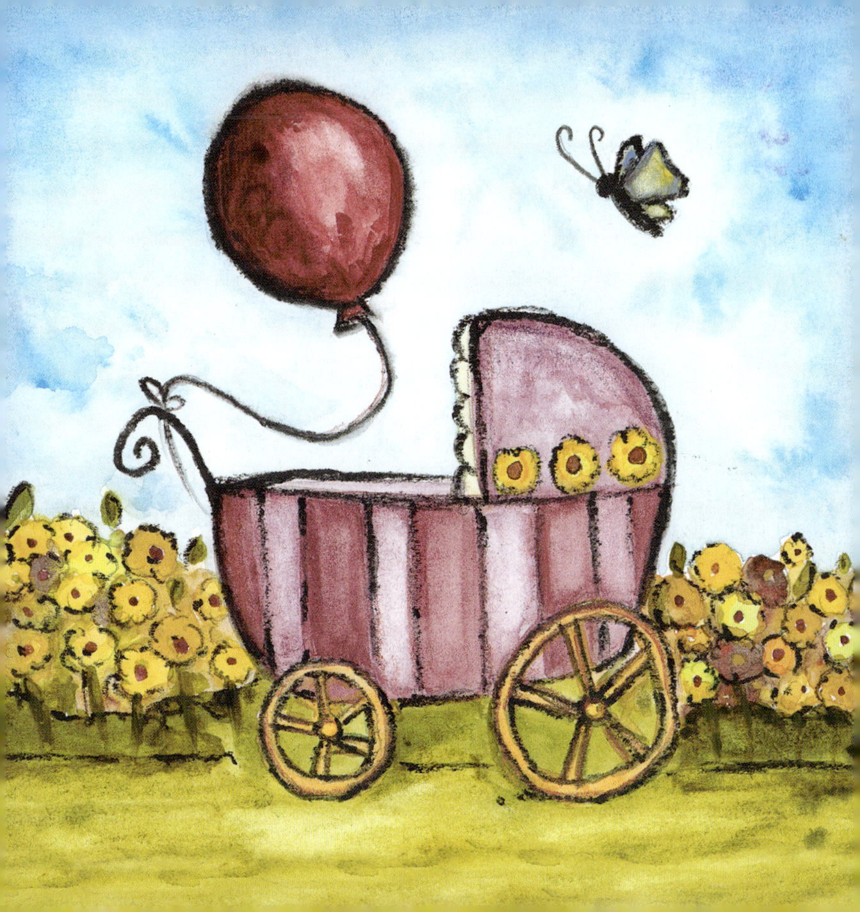

The Lord is good to all,
and His tender mercies
are over all His works.

PSALM 145:9

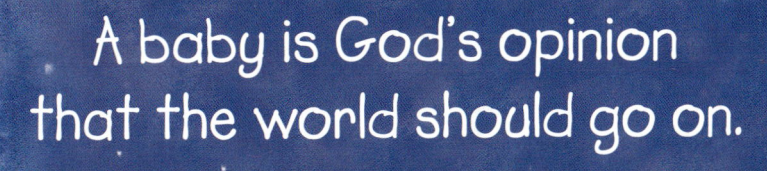

A baby is God's opinion
that the world should go on.

Carl Sandburg

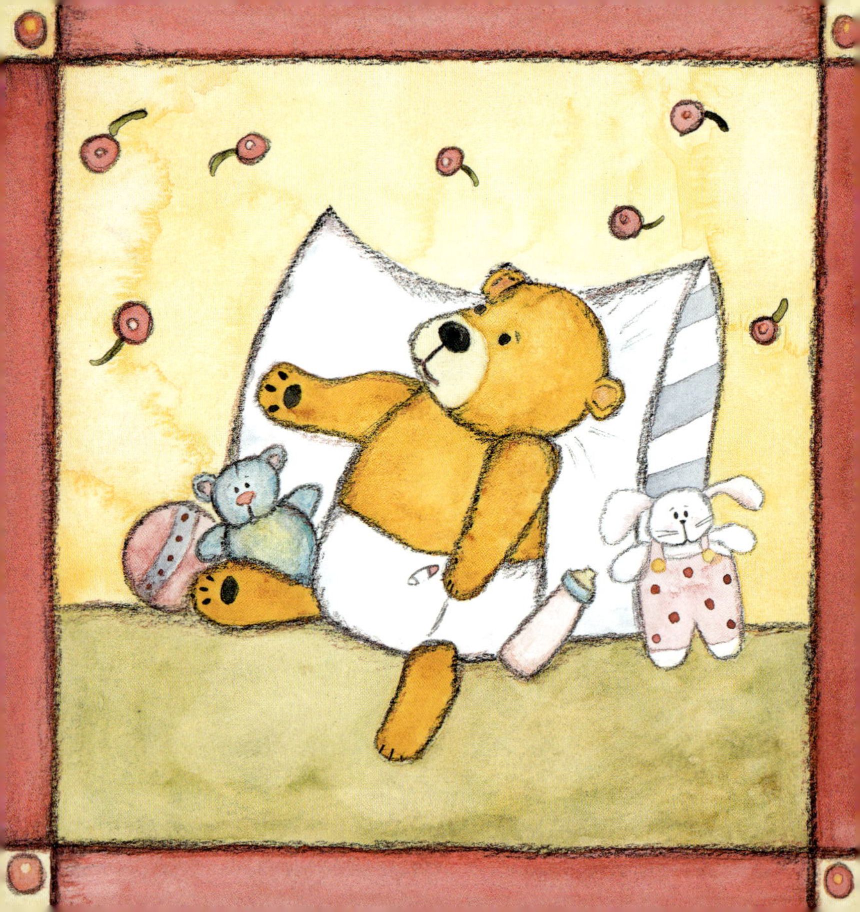

When you lie down, you will not be afraid, yes, you will lie down and your sleep will be sweet.

PROVERBS 3:24

Little ones to Him belong, they are weak but He is strong.

hymn, "Jesus Loves Me"

You formed my inward parts;
You covered me in my mother's womb.

PSALM 139:13

When a baby comes into the world it is as though the pure air of heaven comes along.

Johann Christoph Arnold

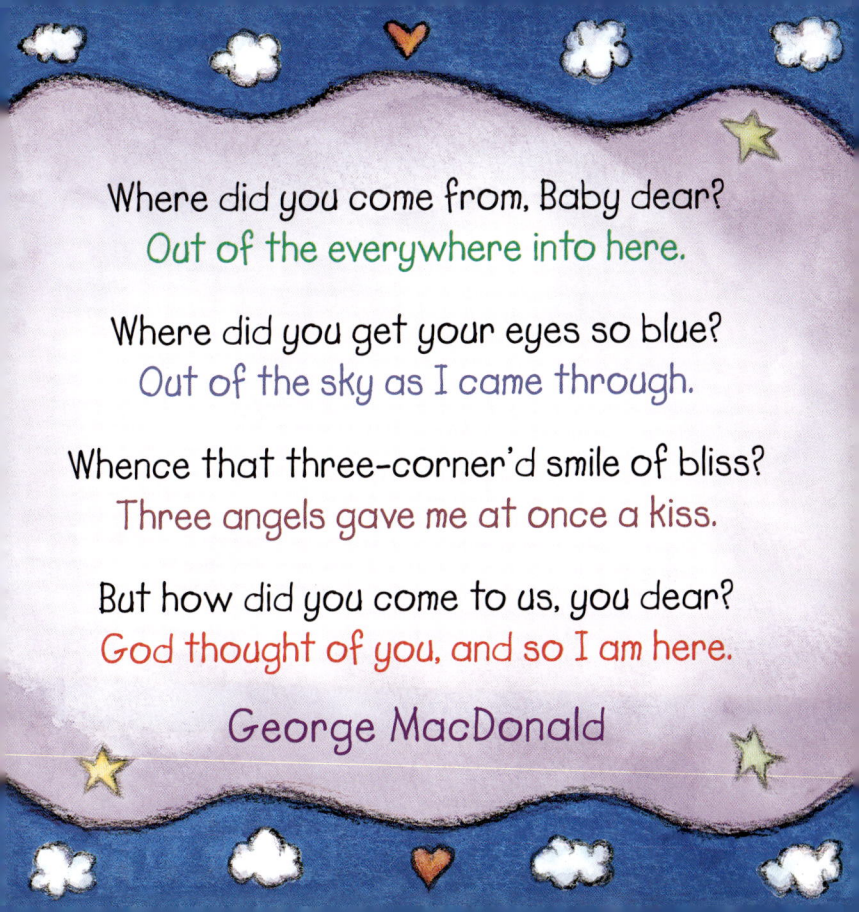

Where did you come from, Baby dear?
Out of the everywhere into here.

Where did you get your eyes so blue?
Out of the sky as I came through.

Whence that three-corner'd smile of bliss?
Three angels gave me at once a kiss.

But how did you come to us, you dear?
God thought of you, and so I am here.

George MacDonald

God shall bless us, and all the ends
of the earth shall fear Him.

PSALMS 67:7

With happy voices ringing
Thy children, LORD, appear;
Their joyous praises bringing
In anthems sweet and clear.

William Tarrant

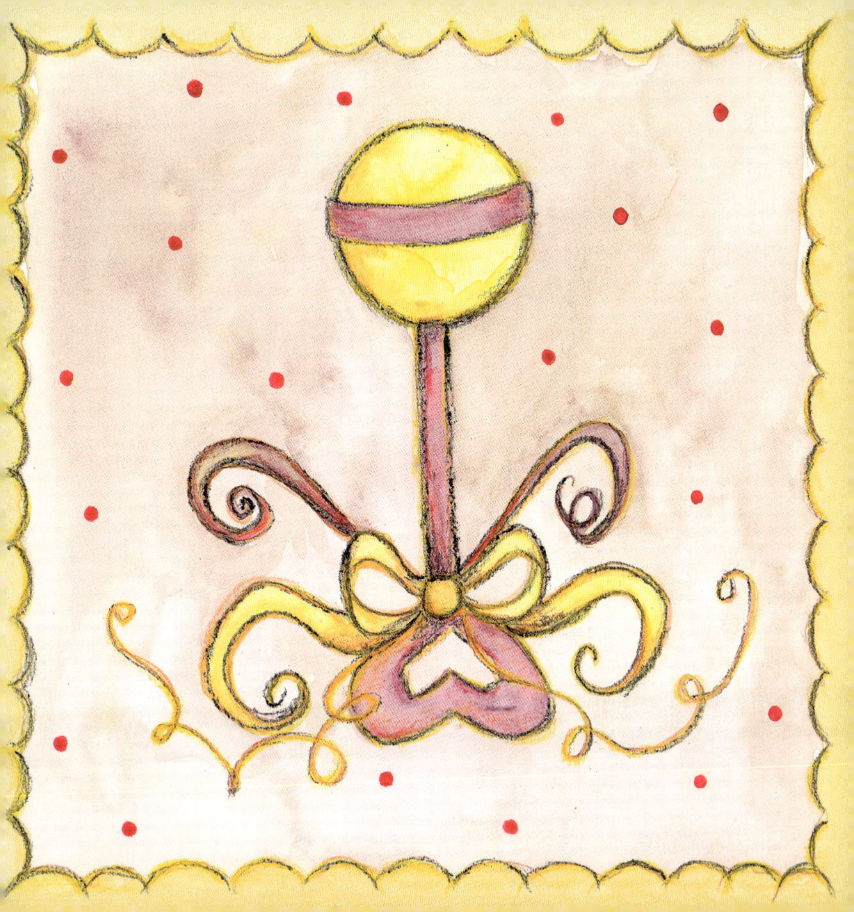

Train up a child in the way he should go,
and when he is old he will not depart from it.

PROVERBS 22:6

There is only one road to the fine character we yearn for our children to have. That is to introduce them to Jesus Christ.

Catherine Marshall

Make me, dear LORD,
polite and kind
To every one, I pray.
And may I ask You
how You find Yourself,
dear LORD, today?

John Bannister Tabb

I will never leave you nor forsake you.

HEBREWS 13:5

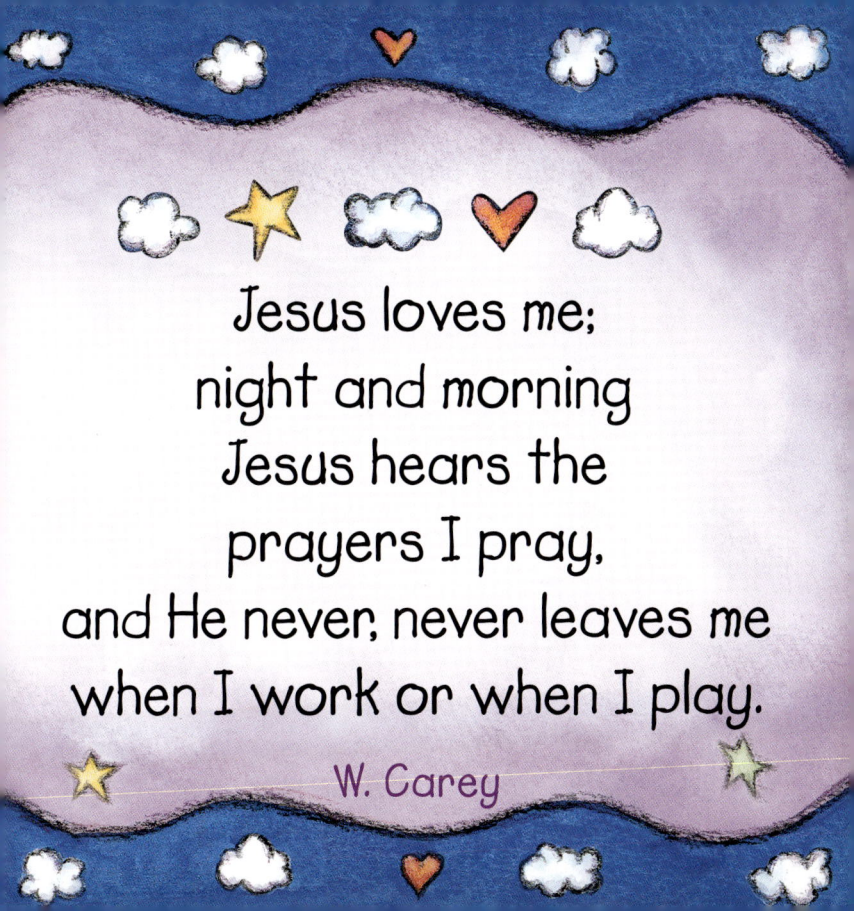

Jesus loves me;
night and morning
Jesus hears the
prayers I pray,
and He never, never leaves me
when I work or when I play.

W. Carey

I am Jesus' little lamb
Ever glad at heart I am;
For my Shepherd
gently guides me,
Knows my need,
and well provides me.

Henrietta L. von Hayn

The LORD is my shepherd; I shall not want.

PSALM 23:1

Wisdom begins in wonder.

Socrates

Children are not things to be molded but are people to be unfolded.

Jess Lair

The LORD will perfect that which concerns me;
Your mercy, O LORD, endures forever.

PSALM 138:8

God's gifts put
man's best dreams
to shame.

Elizabeth Barrett Browning

> I have covered you with the shadow of My hand.
>
> ISAIAH 51:16

At every birth we feel that something of God is born, that something of eternity has come down to us.

Johann Christoph Arnold

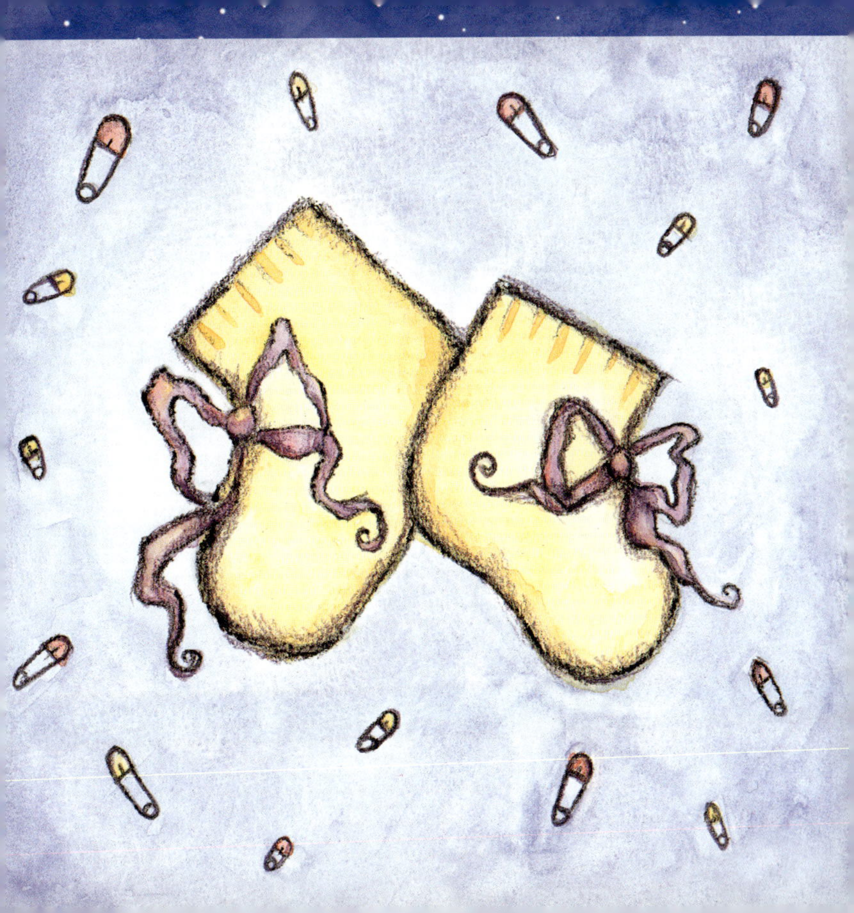

Do not despise one of these little ones,
for I say to you that in heaven their angels
always see the face of My Father who is in heaven.

MATTHEW 18:10

Let us celebrate each child as best, most adored, most surely blessed.

Walter Dean Myers

Those who are loved
much, laugh often.

Anonymous

Tiny yawns and sleepy sighs,
close your precious little eyes
while mother sings
sweet lullabies.

Anonymous

> As the Father loved Me,
> I also have loved you.
>
> JOHN 15:9

The supreme happiness of life is the conviction that we are loved.

Victor Hugo

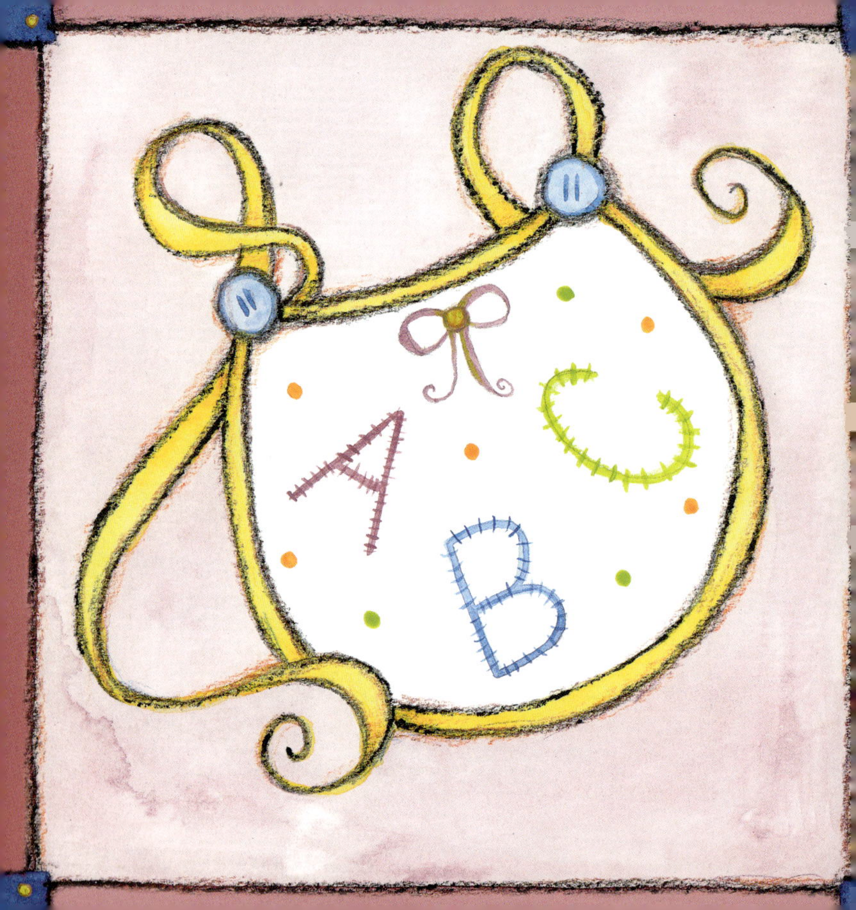
A
B
C

Do not worry, saying "What shall we eat?"...
for your heavenly Father knows
that you need all these things.

MATTHEW 6:31-32

Thank you for the world so sweet. Thank you for the food we eat. Thank you for the birds that sing. Thank you, God, for everything!

R. Leatham

God is love, and he who
abides in love abides in God.

1 JOHN 5:16

Love is shown best in little ways.

Anonymous

He is God; it is He who has made us,
and not we ourselves; we are
His people and the sheep of His pasture.

PSALM 100:3

Jesus is my Shepherd,
I'm His little lamb;
While He guards and guides me,
Safe and glad I am.

Minnie Edington

To kiss a baby's cheek
is to touch an angel's wing.

Anonymous

All children are talented and gifted in some way.

Marti Laney

It takes wisdom to build a house, and understanding to set it on a firm foundation.

PROVERBS 24:3, THE MESSAGE

♥ ♥ ♥

We learn tenderness from our mother and diligence from our dad.

Charles Swindoll

BABY

He will show compassion according to the multitude of His mercies. For He does not afflict willingly, nor grieve the children of men.

LAMENTATIONS 3:32-33

All is well if it is in God's hands.

Charles Spurgeon

Whoever receives one little child
like this in My name receives Me.

MATTHEW 18:5

Little children
are God's life.
There can never
be enough of them.

Mother Teresa

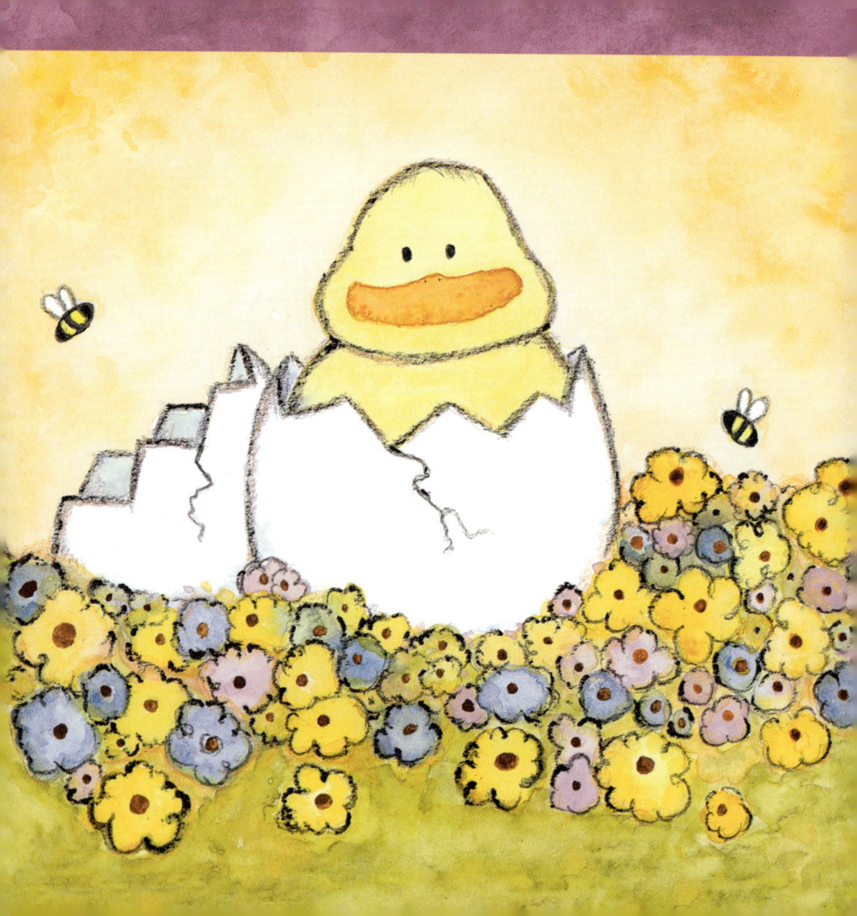

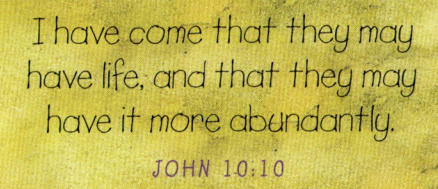

> I have come that they may have life, and that they may have it more abundantly.
>
> JOHN 10:10

For me, life is the most beautiful gift of God to mankind.

Mother Teresa

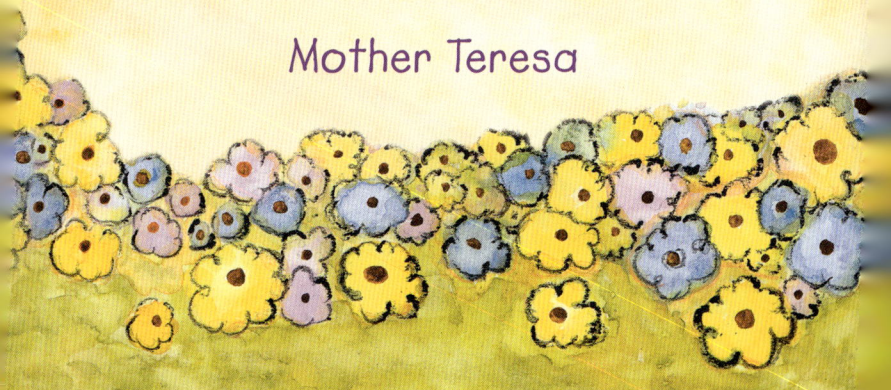

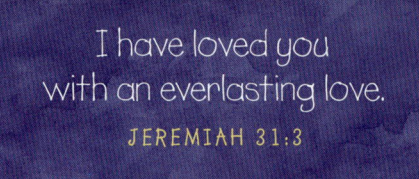

> I have loved you with an everlasting love.
>
> JEREMIAH 31:3

God's love is wonderful because it is unconditional.

Calvin Miller

He shall give His angels charge over you, to keep you in all your ways.

PSALM 91:11

A B C

Through the
long night watches
May Thine angels spread
Their white wings above me,
Watching round my bed.

Sabine Gould

You, O Lord, remain forever;
Your throne from generation to generation.

LAMENTATIONS 5:19

Every baby is a miracle sent from heaven.

Anonymous

From My mother's womb You have been My God.

PSALM 22:10

Thou, my best and kindest Friend,
Thou wilt love me to the end.
Let me love Thee more and more,
Always better than before.

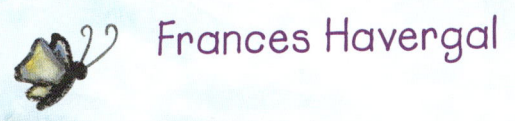

Frances Havergal

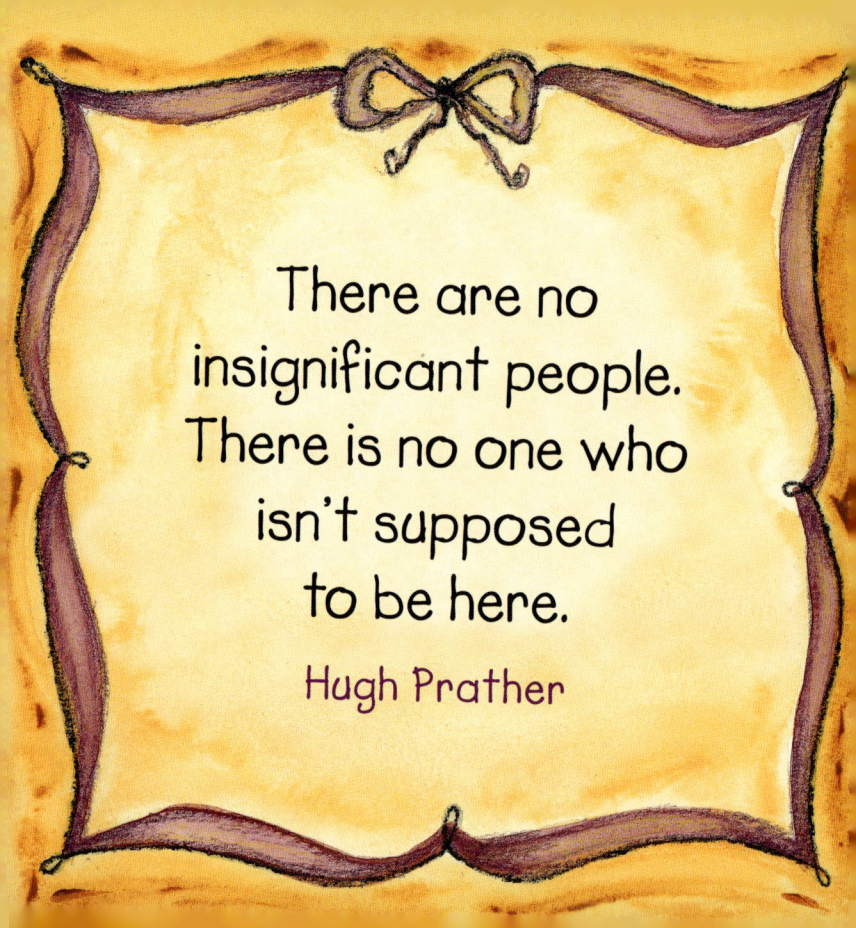

There are no insignificant people. There is no one who isn't supposed to be here.

Hugh Prather

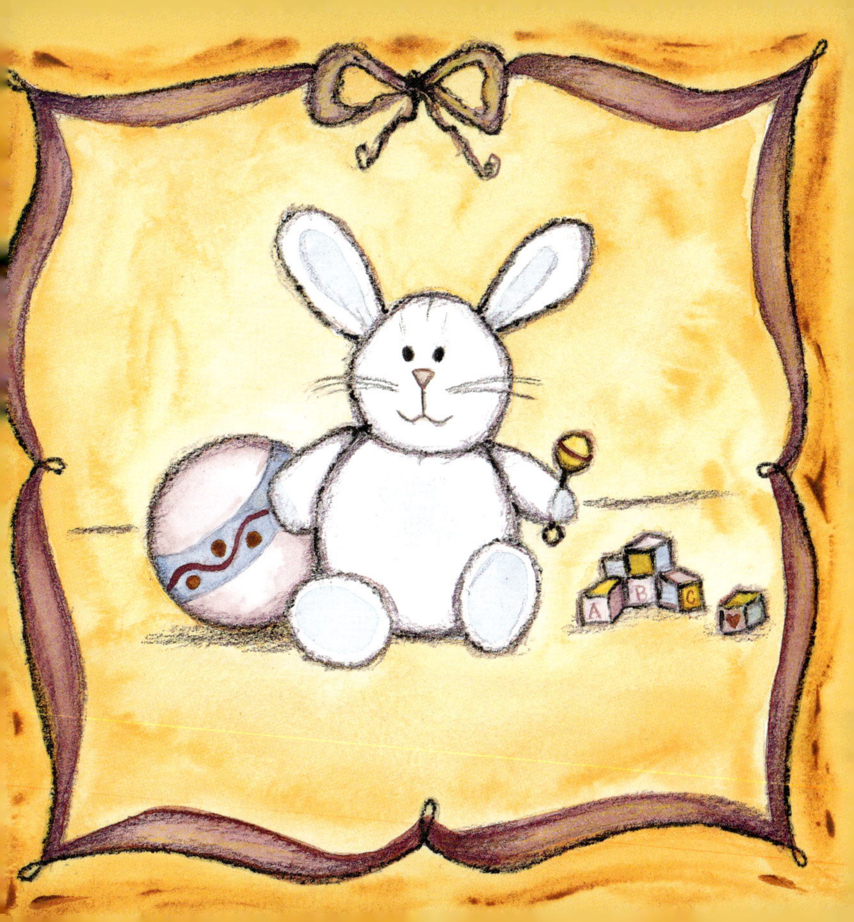
A
B
C

Babies are like daffodils.
Every year new ones
keep popping up.

Barbara Jenkins

> I will give them a heart to know
> Me, that I am the LORD.
>
> JEREMIAH 24:7

Let me learn of Jesus;
He is kind to me;
Once He died to save me,
Nailed upon the tree.

Fanny Crosby

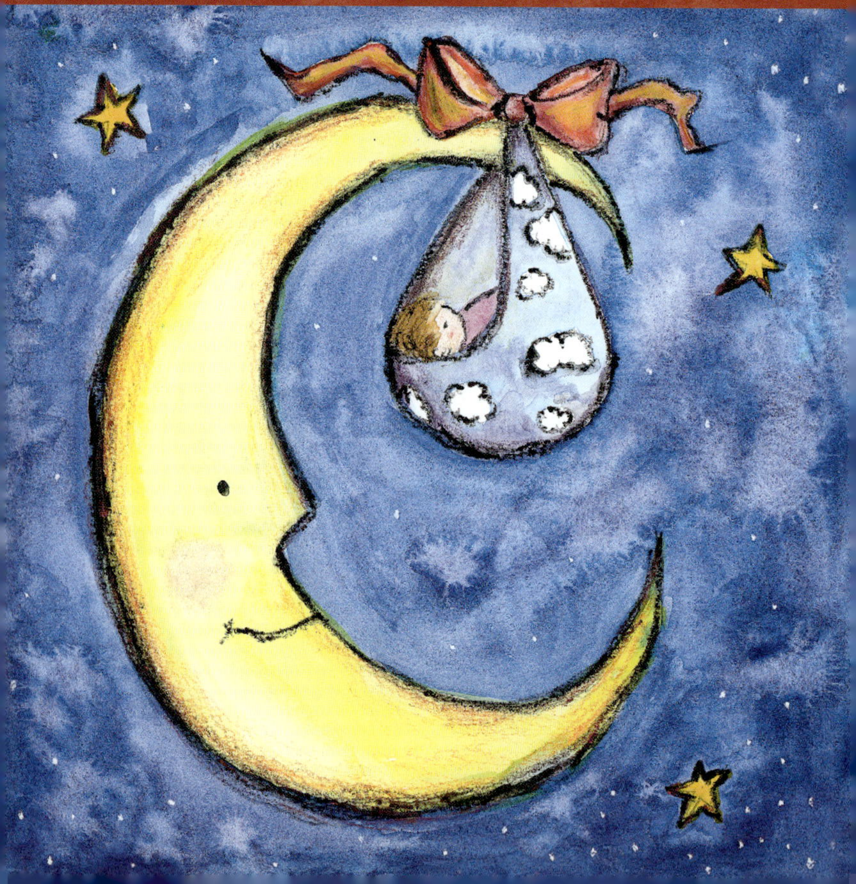

The LORD is the strength of my life,
of whom shall I be afraid?

PSALM 27:1

Lord Jesus,
who does love me,
oh, spread Your
wings above me,
and shield me from alarm!

Paul Gerhardt

As one whom his mother comforts,
so I will comfort you.

ISAIAH 66:13

There was never
a child so lovely
but his mother was glad
to get him to sleep.

Ralph Waldo Emerson

Far away in old Judea
Lived the gentle LORD of love;
Happy children
gathered round Him
Wheresoever He might move,
And they sometimes
left their play
Just to follow Him all day.

Walter J. Mathams

A · B · C ·

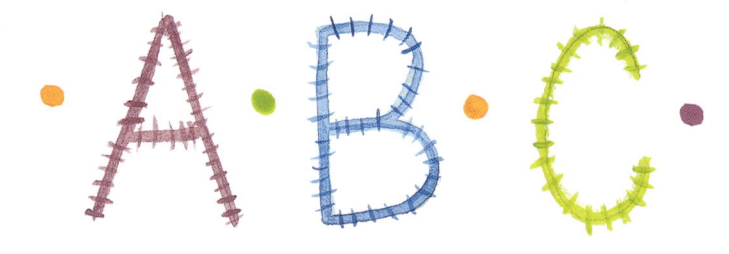

Guard me from sin,
my hand Thou take,
Lord Jesus, Thou my heart do make
A home for Thee until I see
The heavenly home
prepared for me.

Rebecca Weston

> Your right hand has held me up,
> Your gentleness has made me great.
>
> PSALM 18:35

The Bible tells us that each of us matters. We are each the "image of God."

Jonathan Sacks

God so loved the world that He gave His only begotten Son, that whoever believes in Him should not perish but have everlasting life.

JOHN 3:16

Loving Jesus, gentle Lamb In Thy gracious hands I am; Make me, Savior, what Thou art; Live Thyself within my heart.

Charles Wesley

Great events, we often find,
On little things depend,
And very small beginnings
Have oft a might end.

Anonymous

Laugh and grow strong.

St. Ignatius of Loyola

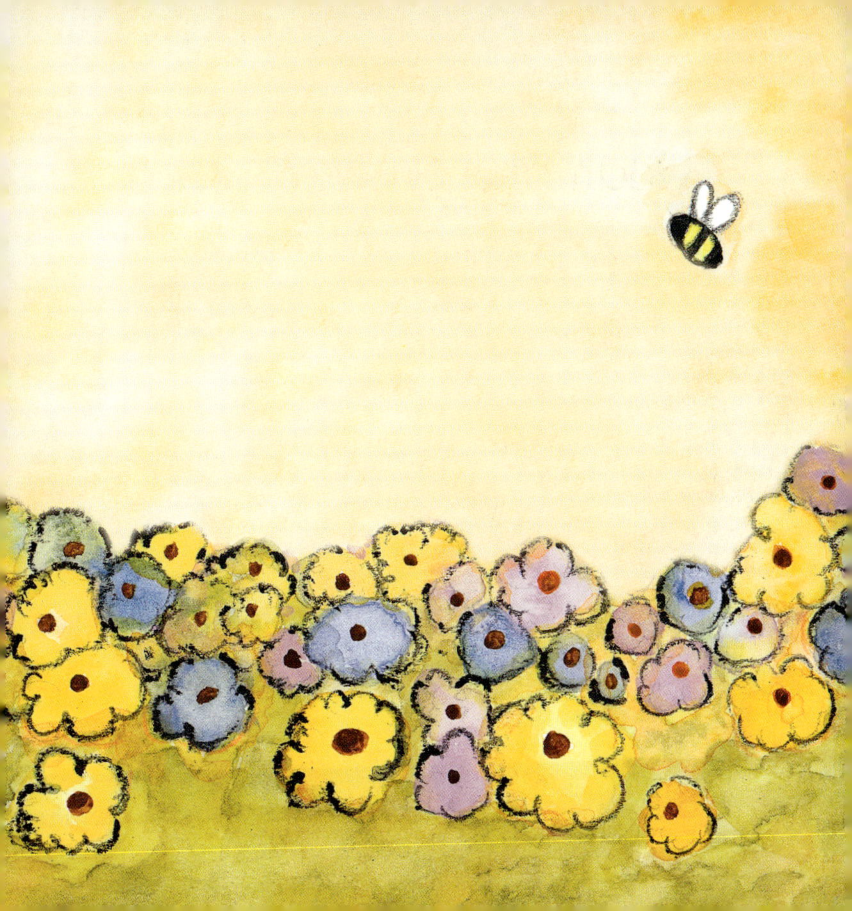